Plant Top Tens

South America's Most Amazing Plants

Chicago, Illinois

© 2008 Raintree
a division of Pearson Inc.
Chicago, Illinois

Customer Service 888-363-4266
Visit our website at www.raintreelibrary.com

Produced for Raintree by Calcium

Editorial: Kate deVilliers and Sarah Eason
Design: Victoria Bevan and Paul Myerscough
Illustrations: Geoff Ward
Picture Research: Maria Joannou
Production: Victoria Fitzgerald

Originated by Modern Age
Printed in China by South China Printing Company

12 11 10 09 08
10 9 8 7 6 5 4 3 2 1

Library of Congress Cataloging-in-Publication Data
Scott, Michael and Royston, Angela.
  Plant top tens. South America / Michael Scott and Angela Royston.
    p. cm.
  Includes bibliographical references and index.
  ISBN 978-1-4109-3144-3 (hc) -- ISBN 978-1-4109-3151-1 (pb) 1. Plants--South America--Juvenile literature. I. Title.
QK241.R69 2008
581.98--dc22

2008001502

Acknowledgments
The authors and publisher are grateful to the following for permission to reproduce copyright material: ©Alamy Images pp. 12 (Mike Lane), 13 (blickwinkel), 16 (Rob Cousins), 21 (Peter Jakubco); ©Corbis pp. 7 (Alison Wright), 19 (Tom Brakefield), 22 (Galen Rowell), 25; ©Dreamstime p. 14 (Anastasia Ryapolova); ©FLPA pp. 8, 27 (Silvestre Silva), 9 (SA Team/Foto Natura), 15 (Fritz Polking); ©Getty Images p. 18 (Minden Pictures/Mark Moffett); ©Robert W. Hoopes, Ph.D. p. 24; ©Istockphoto p. 17; ©NHPA p. 4 (Martin Wendler); ©Photographers Direct p. 26 (Paulo Renato Backes); ©Photolibrary pp. 11 (Roger Rozencwajg/Photononstop), 20 (Oxford Scientific Films/Chris Sharp); ©Shutterstock pp. 10 (Dr. Morley Read), p.23 (Ronnie Howard).

Cover photograph of a Victoria water lily, reproduced with permission of Ardea/Chris Martin Bahr.

Every effort has been made to contact copyright holders of any material reproduced in this book. Any omissions will be rectified in subsequent printings if notice is given to the publishers.

Disclaimer
All the Internet addresses (URLs) given in this book were valid at time of going to press. However, due to the dynamic nature of the Internet, some addresses may have changed, or sites may have changed or ceased to exist since publication. While the author and publishers regret any inconvenience this may cause readers, no responsibility for any such changes can be accepted by either the author or the publishers. It is recommended that adults supervise children on the Internet.

Contents

Some words are printed in bold, **like this**. You can find out what they mean on page 31 in the Glossary.

South America

South America stretches from the Caribbean Sea in the north almost to **Antarctica** in the south. In the north it includes the mighty Amazon River, the largest river in the world. An enormous **rain forest** grows on each side of the river. South of the rain forest is a huge area of grassland called the **pampas**. The high Andes Mountains stretch all the way down the west coast of South America.

The Amazon Rain Forest is the largest rain forest in the world.

Species

A species is a particular type of plant or animal. One-fifth of all the species of flowering plants in the world grow in the Amazon Rain Forest.

The huge Amazon Rain Forest is found in South America.

Galapagos
Islands

South America

Atlantic Ocean

N
W—E
S

Amazon River

Amazon
Rain Forest

Andes

SOUTH AMERICA

Lake Titicaca

Panantal
Swamps

Atacama Desert

Pacific Ocean

Key
rain forest
desert
grassland
mountains
swamp
borderlines

Pampas

0   500 miles
0   500 kilometers

Tierra del Fuego

Different habitats

Rain forest, grassland, and mountains are all
different types of **habitat**. A habitat includes the
plants that grow there and the animals that live
there. Desert and **peat bog** are two other habitats
in South America. The peat bogs are at the
southern tip. There the weather is almost as cold
as in Antarctica.

Curare Vine

A curare vine grows from a **seed** in the soil of the rain forest. Rain forest trees grow so tall and so close together that very little light reaches the ground. The vine grows fast, scrambling up the trunks of the trees toward the sunlight. It has a trick to help it survive. The **sap** of the vine is poisonous. Insects and larger animals know not to eat it.

Photosynthesis

Plants need light to survive. They make sugar using the energy of sunlight and a green chemical in their leaves. The process is called **photosynthesis**.

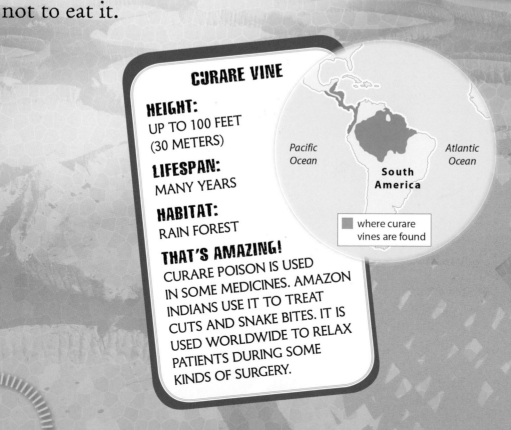

CURARE VINE

HEIGHT:
UP TO 100 FEET
(30 METERS)

LIFESPAN:
MANY YEARS

HABITAT:
RAIN FOREST

THAT'S AMAZING!
CURARE POISON IS USED IN SOME MEDICINES. AMAZON INDIANS USE IT TO TREAT CUTS AND SNAKE BITES. IT IS USED WORLDWIDE TO RELAX PATIENTS DURING SOME KINDS OF SURGERY.

Pacific Ocean

Atlantic Ocean

South America

where curare vines are found

Poison arrow

Curare is so poisonous that Amazon Indians have used it for hundreds of years to help them hunt animals. They dip the tips of their darts in it. When a dart pierces an animal, the poison **paralyzes** the animal so it cannot escape.

Amazon Indians blow poisoned darts through a wooden tube. The poison is curare.

Brazil Nut Tree

The Brazil nut tree is one of the tallest trees in the Amazon Rain Forest. It grows so tall that it reaches above the rest of the forest. This helps it get plenty of sunlight. The fruit of a Brazil nut tree is enormous. The outer layer is hard wood. Inside are 10 to 20 seeds, which we call Brazil nuts. They fit together like the pieces of an orange.

BRAZIL NUT TREE

HEIGHT:
UP TO 164 FEET (50 METERS)

LIFESPAN:
AROUND 500 YEARS

HABITAT:
AMAZON RAIN FOREST

THAT'S AMAZING!
THE OUTER LAYER OF THE BRAZIL NUT FRUIT IS SO TOUGH THAT EVEN PEOPLE FIND IT DIFFICULT TO BREAK IT OPEN.

South America

Pacific Ocean

Atlantic Ocean

■ where Brazil nut trees are found

Brazil nut tree fruit is as big and heavy as a cannonball.

An agouti has very sharp teeth that can gnaw into the fruit of a Brazil nut tree.

From seed to tree

Agoutis are the only animals that can gnaw through the outer wooden shell of a Brazil nut fruit. They eat a few seeds, then bury some for later. They often forget where they buried them, and so these seeds begin to grow! They will only grow well in bright sunlight, however. When an old tree falls over, it leaves a brightly lit gap on the rain forest floor where a new tree can grow.

Cacao Tree

Chocolate is made from cocoa beans. They are the seeds of cacao trees. Cacao trees first grew in the rain forest, but people now plant them in other warm, wet places. The beans form inside large **pods** that grow straight out of the branches and trunk. They look as if they have been stuck on to the tree! People collect the pods to make chocolate.

Cocoa beans ripen inside large pods.

Cocoa pods

Inside the pods, the cocoa beans are surrounded by soft **pulp**. Monkeys like to eat this pulp. The beans pass through their bodies and fall on to the ground. Some of them grow into new trees. If the pods are not eaten or collected, they stay on the tree. Tiny flies nest in the rotting pods. When new flowers open, the flies carry **pollen** from one flower to another. The flowers then make more cocoa pods.

Today, most cacao trees are specially planted. The beans are made into chocolate.

CACAO TREE

HEIGHT:
UP TO 26 FEET (8 METERS)

LIFESPAN:
UP TO 100 YEARS

HABITAT:
RAIN FOREST

THAT'S AMAZING!
HUNDREDS OF YEARS AGO, THE MAYA PEOPLE OF MEXICO USED COCOA BEANS AS MONEY AND TO MAKE A DRINK. THE BEANS WERE SO VALUABLE THAT ONLY THE RULERS WERE ALLOWED TO DRINK COCOA!

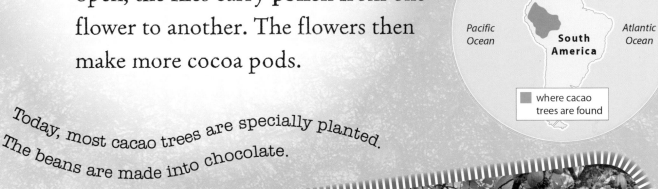

Pacific Ocean

South America

Atlantic Ocean

where cacao trees are found

Rubber Tree

Rubber trees grow all year round in the rain forest. The juice (sap) of rubber trees is very special. It is a white milky liquid called **latex**. When latex dries it becomes a rubbery solid. Latex may help the plant in two ways. It may stop insects drilling into the trunk to eat the wood, and it may help to repair the trunk if it is damaged.

Sap
Sap is like blood to a plant. It takes sugar, **nutrients**, and water to every part of the plant.

Rubber trees grow best in places that are hot.

Collecting sap

People grow rubber trees to collect their sap. Every two days they make a cut in the bark and collect the latex in cups. This is called **tapping**. The latex is made into rubber. Each time a tree is tapped, it gives enough latex to make almost 2 ounces (50 grams) of solid rubber.

RUBBER TREE

HEIGHT:
UP TO 100 FEET (30 METERS)

LIFESPAN:
MORE THAN 30 YEARS

HABITAT:
RAIN FOREST

THAT'S AMAZING!
RUBBER IS MADE INTO TIRES FOR RACING CARS AND AIRPLANES. THIS IS BECAUSE RUBBER DOES NOT GET HOT WHEN THE CAR OR AIRPLANE BRAKES.

Pacific Ocean

Atlantic Ocean

South America

where rubber trees are found

Sap from the rubber tree runs down the cut and collects in a cup.

Victoria Water Lily

The Victoria water lily grows in lakes. It has the largest leaves of any floating plant in the world. The underside of the leaf has thick, strong **veins** that spread out like a fan. They make the leaf so strong that a small child can sit on it!

Victoria water lilies grow in lakes beside the Amazon River.

Lily trotters build their nests on the giant leaves of Victoria water lilies. Their eggs are safe there from **predators**.

Trapping beetles

Victoria water lilies use beetles to carry pollen from one flower to another. The beetles crawl into the center of the flower. The flower then snaps shut. It traps the beetles and dusts them with pollen. The next night the flower opens and the beetles carry the pollen to another flower. The pollen **fertilizes** the seeds of the next flower. The flower then dies and is pulled under the water. When the seeds are ripe, they float to the surface.

VICTORIA WATER LILY

HEIGHT:
UP TO 13 FEET (4 METERS) FROM THE BOTTOM OF THE LAKE

LIFESPAN:
LESS THAN A YEAR

HABITAT:
LAKES AROUND THE AMAZON RIVER

THAT'S AMAZING!
THE LEAF OF A VICTORIA WATER LILY IS AS BIG AS A DOUBLE BED.

South America

Pacific Ocean

Atlantic Ocean

where Victoria water lilies are found

Ruby-Lipped Cattleya Orchid

Ruby-lipped cattleya orchids grow in thick rain forests where most plants struggle upward to reach the light. This orchid, however, has a special trick. Instead of growing from the ground, its seeds start growing high in the branches of trees. The orchid's roots dangle down from the branch. They are covered with a spongy material that soaks in water from the damp air.

These orchids grow high in the branches of rain forest trees.

Roots

Roots usually take in water and nutrients from the soil. Roots that grow in the soil also anchor the plant in the ground.

Storing water

Ruby-lipped cattleya orchids have special containers for storing water. These look like small bulbs on the plant's **stem**. Each plant has up to 30 large, brightly colored flowers. They grow in a cluster at the tip of the flower stem.

RUBY-LIPPED CATTLEYA ORCHID

HEIGHT:
UP TO 18 INCHES
(46 CENTIMETERS)

LIFESPAN:
USUALLY 3–5 YEARS

HABITAT:
MOUNTAIN RAIN FOREST

THAT'S AMAZING!
EUROPEANS DISCOVERED RUBY-LIPPED CATTLEYA ORCHIDS BY ACCIDENT NEARLY 200 YEARS AGO. A SCIENTIST USED THE SPONGY ROOTS TO PACK AROUND OTHER PLANTS. WHEN THE ROOT WAS PLANTED, IT GREW INTO A BEAUTIFUL FLOWERING PLANT!

Pacific Ocean

South America

Atlantic Ocean

■ where ruby-lipped cattleya orchids are found

Ruby-lipped cattleya orchid flowers are red, white, or pink.

Imperial Bromeliad

Imperial bromeliads grow in cracks on steep, rocky cliffs. When it rains, the water runs straight down the cliff. Instead of taking in water through its roots, an imperial bromeliad has its own way of storing water. Its long leaves grow in a tight circle in the middle of the plant. They form a tank that holds water.

Few plants can grow on a rocky cliff, but imperial bromeliads grow very big there.

Pacific Ocean

South America

Atlantic Ocean

where imperial bromeliads are found

Scaly leaves

The leaves of imperial bromeliads have scales
on them. These scales open to let the plant
take in water. The bromeliad's tall flower grows
up through the center of the tank. Other kinds
of tank bromeliad grow high in rain forest
trees. Tree frogs lay eggs in their tanks of water.
The eggs hatch into tadpoles that live in the
water until they have grown into frogs.

Monkey-Puzzle Tree

Monkey-puzzle trees grow as far south as any other tree in the world. They grow on the slopes of the Andes Mountains, where **lava** from **volcanoes** makes the soil rich in nutrients. In winter the trees are covered by thick snow. They have deep roots that find water even when the ground above is frozen. The trees grow very slowly. This allows them to save energy and helps them to survive.

Monkey-puzzle trees are sometimes called Chile pines.

MONKEY-PUZZLE TREE

HEIGHT:
UP TO 164 FEET (50 METERS)

LIFESPAN:
UP TO 1,000 YEARS

HABITAT:
MOUNTAIN FORESTS

THAT'S AMAZING!
FORESTS OF MONKEY-PUZZLE TREES WERE GROWING IN SOUTH AMERICA 70 MILLION YEARS AGO. DINOSAURS MAY HAVE SCRATCHED THEIR BACKS AGAINST THEM!

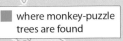

where monkey-puzzle trees are found

Pacific Ocean

South America

Atlantic Ocean

Prickly tree

The leaves of the monkey-puzzle tree are stiff needles with sharp points and edges. They grow one over the other to form a spiky spiral. Someone once said a monkey would be puzzled how to climb the prickly branches. That is how the tree got its name! In fact, no monkeys live where monkey-puzzle trees grow wild.

The cones of a monkey-puzzle tree are massive. They are up to 7 inches (19 centimeters) long.

Conifers
Monkey-puzzle trees are **conifers**. They have needles instead of leaves, and they produce their seeds in **cones**.

Giant Puya

Giant puyas have the biggest spikes of flowers in the world. The flower spikes look like white, feathery brushes. A single spike has up to 8,000 flowers! The spikes tower above the tough, leathery leaves. The leaves are covered with sharp spines that stop animals from eating them. Giant puyas grow high in the Andes Mountains, where few other plants can grow.

The giant puya's flowers are much taller than a person!

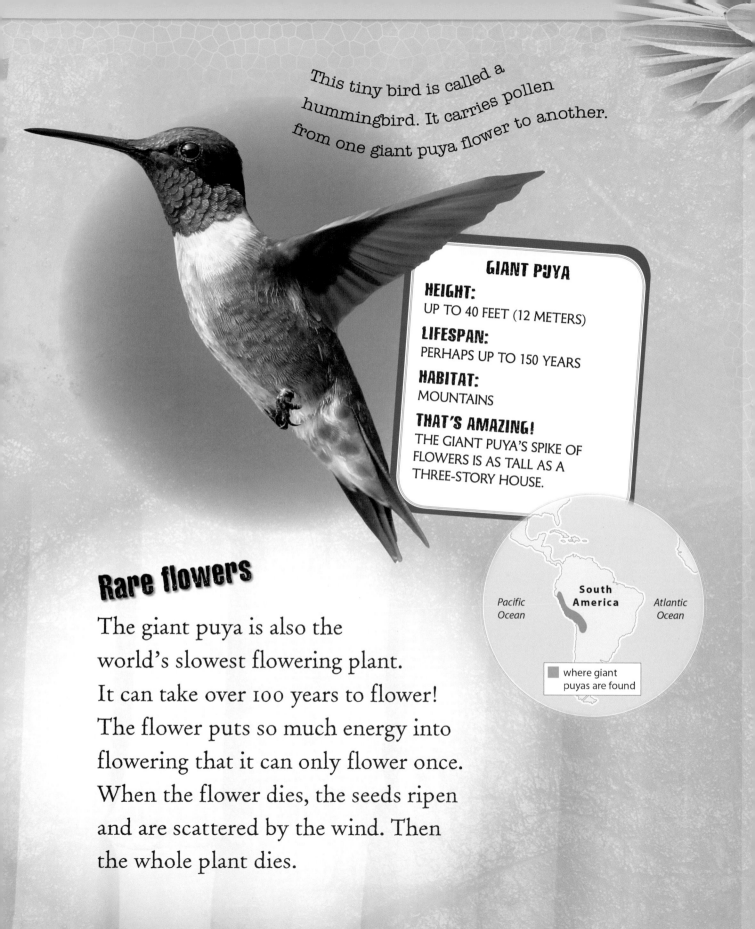

This tiny bird is called a hummingbird. It carries pollen from one giant puya flower to another.

GIANT PUYA

HEIGHT:
UP TO 40 FEET (12 METERS)

LIFESPAN:
PERHAPS UP TO 150 YEARS

HABITAT:
MOUNTAINS

THAT'S AMAZING!
THE GIANT PUYA'S SPIKE OF FLOWERS IS AS TALL AS A THREE-STORY HOUSE.

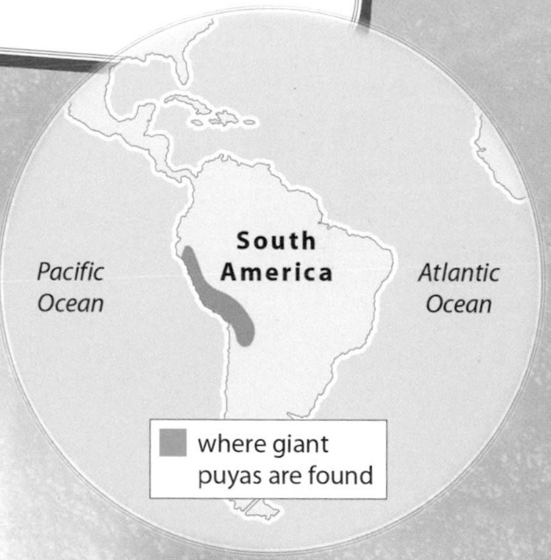
South America
Pacific Ocean
Atlantic Ocean
where giant puyas are found

Rare flowers

The giant puya is also the world's slowest flowering plant. It can take over 100 years to flower! The flower puts so much energy into flowering that it can only flower once. When the flower dies, the seeds ripen and are scattered by the wind. Then the whole plant dies.

Potato

Potatoes have been grown for food for 13,000 years, but they grew only in the Andes Mountains until 500 years ago. Today, they are grown in countries all over the world. Potatoes grow well in many kinds of soil. Potatoes are **tubers**. This means that they are the swollen ends of underground stems.

Tubers

Tubers are a store of energy and nutrients. In winter the stem and leaves of the plant die. In spring the tuber produces a new stem and the plant grows again. Sweet potatoes and Jerusalem artichokes are tubers, too.

Potatoes first grew high in the Andes Mountains, where few other plants grow.

Potato eyes

Each potato has buds, which are often called "eyes." New stems sprout from the eyes and push up through the soil. They form leaves and flowers. The leaves and other green parts of potato plants are poisonous. The poison stops animals from eating the plant. Fresh potatoes are not poisonous, however. They are good to eat once they are cooked.

POTATO

SIZE:
UP TO 3.3 FEET
(1 METER) HIGH

LIFESPAN:
MANY YEARS

HABITAT:
MOUNTAINS

THAT'S AMAZING!
POTATOES LEFT OUT IN THE SUN TURN GREEN. THEY BECOME POISONOUS LIKE THE REST OF THE PLANT.

where potatoes are found

Pacific Ocean

South America

Atlantic Ocean

Potatoes grow in soil at the end of stems under the ground.

Plants in Danger

Some of the plants that grow in South America are in danger of becoming **extinct** in the wild. This means that soon there will be none left.

More and more of the land where bahia discocactus plants grow is being used for other things. Some of it is being built on. Some is being used as farmland. A large area was made into a lake. People need to keep some land as a special place for bahia discocactus plants to grow.

Bahia discocactus plants grow on gravelly ground beside rivers.

If these paraná pines disappear from the wild, the animals that live on them could disappear, too.

Plants become endangered for many reasons. There used to be huge forests of paraná pines in South America, but now only one-fifth of them remain. The rest have been cut down, with their wood used as timber. It is made into furniture, doors, windows, and other things that people use. People also collect and eat the seeds of paraná pines. They do not leave behind many seeds to grow into new trees.

Plant Facts and Figures

There are millions of different kinds of plant growing all over the world. The place where a plant lives is called its habitat. Plants have special features, such as flowers, leaves, and stems. These features allow plants to survive in their habitats. Which plant do you think is the most amazing?

CURARE VINE

HEIGHT:
UP TO 100 FEET (30 METERS)

LIFESPAN:
MANY YEARS

HABITAT:
RAIN FOREST

THAT'S AMAZING!
CURARE POISON IS USED IN SOME MEDICINES. AMAZON INDIANS USE IT TO TREAT CUTS AND SNAKE BITES. IT IS USED WORLDWIDE TO RELAX PATIENTS DURING SOME KINDS OF SURGERY.

BRAZIL NUT TREE

HEIGHT:
UP TO 164 FEET (50 METERS)

LIFESPAN:
500 YEARS

HABITAT:
AMAZON RAIN FOREST

THAT'S AMAZING!
THE OUTER LAYER OF THE BRAZIL NUT FRUIT IS SO TOUGH THAT EVEN PEOPLE FIND IT DIFFICULT TO BREAK IT OPEN.

CACAO TREE

HEIGHT:
UP TO 26 FEET (8 METERS)

LIFESPAN:
UP TO 100 YEARS

HABITAT:
RAIN FOREST

THAT'S AMAZING!
HUNDREDS OF YEARS AGO, THE MAYA PEOPLE OF MEXICO USED COCOA BEANS AS MONEY AND TO MAKE A DRINK. THE BEANS WERE SO VALUABLE THAT ONLY THE RULERS WERE ALLOWED TO DRINK COCOA!

RUBBER TREE

HEIGHT:
UP TO 100 FEET (30 METERS)

LIFESPAN:
MORE THAN 30 YEARS

HABITAT:
RAIN FOREST

THAT'S AMAZING!
RUBBER IS MADE INTO TIRES FOR RACING CARS AND AIRPLANES. THIS IS BECAUSE RUBBER DOES NOT GET HOT WHEN THE CAR OR AIRPLANE BRAKES.

VICTORIA WATER LILY

HEIGHT:
UP TO 13 FEET (4 METERS)
FROM THE BOTTOM OF
THE LAKE

LIFESPAN:
LESS THAN A YEAR

HABITAT:
LAKES AROUND THE
AMAZON RIVER

THAT'S AMAZING!
THE LEAF OF A VICTORIA
WATER LILY IS AS BIG AS A
DOUBLE BED.

RUBY-LIPPED CATTLEYA ORCHID

HEIGHT:
UP TO 18 INCHES
(46 CENTIMETERS)

LIFESPAN:
USUALLY 3–5 YEARS

HABITAT:
MOUNTAIN RAIN FOREST

THAT'S AMAZING!
EUROPEANS DISCOVERED
RUBY-LIPPED CATTLEYA
ORCHIDS BY ACCIDENT
NEARLY 200 YEARS AGO.
A SCIENTIST USED THE
SPONGY ROOTS TO
PACK AROUND OTHER
PLANTS. WHEN THE
ROOT WAS PLANTED, IT
GREW INTO A BEAUTIFUL
FLOWERING PLANT!

IMPERIAL BROMELIAD

HEIGHT:
FLOWER IS 10–16 FEET
(3–5 METERS)

LIFESPAN:
10 YEARS OR MORE

HABITAT:
ROCKY MOUNTAIN CLIFFS

THAT'S AMAZING!
THE IMPERIAL BROMELIAD
IS ONE OF THE LARGEST
TANK BROMELIADS. ITS
CIRCLE OF LEAVES IS AS BIG
AS A TRUCK'S TIRE!

MONKEY-PUZZLE TREE

HEIGHT:
UP TO 164 FEET (50 METERS)

LIFESPAN:
UP TO 1,000 YEARS

HABITAT:
MOUNTAIN FORESTS

THAT'S AMAZING!
FORESTS OF MONKEY-
PUZZLE TREES WERE
GROWING IN SOUTH
AMERICA 70 MILLION YEARS
AGO. DINOSAURS MAY
HAVE SCRATCHED THEIR
BACKS AGAINST THEM!

GIANT PUYA

HEIGHT:
UP TO 40 FEET (12 METERS)

LIFESPAN:
PERHAPS UP TO 150 YEARS

HABITAT:
MOUNTAINS

THAT'S AMAZING!
THE GIANT PUYA'S SPIKE
OF FLOWERS IS AS TALL AS
A THREE-STORY HOUSE.

POTATO

SIZE:
UP TO 3.3 FEET (1 METER)
HIGH

LIFESPAN:
MANY YEARS

HABITAT:
MOUNTAINS

THAT'S AMAZING!
POTATOES LEFT OUT IN
THE SUN TURN GREEN.
THEY BECOME POISONOUS
LIKE THE REST OF
THE PLANT.

Find Out More

Books to read

Blackaby, Susan. *The World's Largest Plants*. Minneapolis: Picture Window, 2003.

Boothroyd, Jennifer. *Plants and the Environment*. Minneapolis: Lerner, 2007.

Chinery, Michael. *Plants and Planteaters (Secrets of the Rain forest)*. New York: Crabtree, 2000.

Fowler, Allan. *Plants That Eat Animals*. New York: Children's Press, 2001.

Ganeri, Anita. *Plant Life Cycles*. Chicago: Heinemann Library, 2005.

Websites

www.abcteach.com/Rain forestFacts/plants.htm
Discover more about the amazing plants of the South American rain forests.

www.botany.org/Carnivorous_Plants/
Find out all about plants that eat flesh!

www.junglephotos.com/amazon/amplants/amplants.shtml
Click on photographs to learn about plants of the Amazon rain forest.

www.mbgnet.net/bioplants/adapt.html
Discover how plants adapt to different habitats, including deserts, grasslands, tropical rain forests, temperate forests, tundra, and water.

Glossary

Antarctica frozen land that surrounds the South Pole

cone hard, dry fruit of a conifer tree that carries the seeds

conifer tree that produces its seeds in cones

extinct no longer in existence

fertilize join a grain of pollen with an ovule (plant egg) so that it can become a ripe seed

habitat place in the wild where particular types of plant grow and particular types of animal live

latex sap from a rubber tree

lava melted, runny rock that bursts out of volcanoes. When it cools it makes the soil good for plants to grow in.

nutrient part of food that is needed for health

pampas areas of grassland in South America where few trees grow

paralyze make a living thing unable to move

peat bog soft, wet ground where dead plants have turned into a material called peat

photosynthesis process through which plants make their food using the energy of sunlight

pod container that holds seeds

pollen yellow dust made by flowers

predator animal that hunts other animals for food

pulp soft part of a fruit or vegetable

rain forest forest where it rains almost every day and where plants and trees grow close together

sap plant juice made up mainly of water and sugar

seed part of a plant that can grow into a new plant

stem part of a plant on which leaves or a flower grow

tapping making a cut in bark so that the sap can flow out

tuber swollen part of an underground stem that grows into a new plant

vein tube in a living thing that carries liquid, such as sap or blood

volcano place on the surface of Earth where hot melted rock from inside Earth bursts out

Index